Bags of SHOWBIZ for violin

Arranged and written by
Mary Cohen

© 2009 by Faber Music Ltd
This edition first published in 2009
Bloomsbury House 74–77 Great Russell Street London WC1B 3DA
Music processed by Jeanne Roberts
Cover designed by Lydia Merrills-Ashcroft
Illustration by Andy Cooke
Printed in England by Caligraving Ltd
All rights reserved

ISBN10: 0-571-53294-2
EAN13: 978-0-571-53294-0

To buy Faber Music publications or to find out about the full range of titles available
please contact your local music retailer or Faber Music sales enquiries:

Faber Music Ltd, Burnt Mill, Elizabeth Way, Harlow CM20 2HX
Tel: +44 (0) 1279 82 89 82   Fax: +44 (0) 1279 82 89 83
sales@fabermusic.com   fabermusic.com

FABER ff MUSIC

Foreword

Bags of Showbiz is full of film, pop, TV and show tunes that my pupils whistle, hum and sing when they are chilling out. As well as being terrific to play, this collection introduces lots of great rhythms, moods and styles that will help to develop reading skills and technique. It's perfect for playing for fun or in concerts—a book to dip into again and again.

Contents

Supercalifragilisticexpialidocious

Words and Music by
Richard Sherman and Robert Sherman

Chitty chitty bang bang

Words and Music by
Richard Sherman and Robert Sherman

Over the rainbow (from 'The Wizard of Oz')

Words by E. Y. Harburg
Music by Harold Arlen

The lady is a tramp

Words by Lorenz Hart
Music by Richard Rodgers

Dancing on ice

Mary Cohen

We're all in this together (from 'High School Musical')

Words and Music by Matthew Gerrard and Robbie Nevil

Beauty and the beast

Words by Howard Ashman
Music by Alan Menken

I wonder... will I get this role?

Shyly, but full of hope

Mary Cohen

The entertainer

Very stylish

Scott Joplin

Hedwig's theme (from 'Harry Potter and the Philosopher's Stone')

Music by John Williams

Razzamatazz

Mary Cohen

In the bright lights

All lit up!

Mary Cohen

Dr Who

Music by Ron Grainer

There's no business like show business

Words and Music by Irving Berlin

It's the end of the show!

Mary Cohen

The Pink Panther theme

Music by Henry Mancini

Food, glorious food (from 'Oliver!')

Words and Music by Lionel Bart

Get ready! We're ready!

Mary Cohen

James Bond theme

With a glint of steel

Music by Monty Norman

Star quality!

Mary Cohen

Dazzlingly

I could have danced all night (from 'My Fair Lady')

Words by Alan Jay Lerner
Music by Frederick Loewe

With terrific enthusiasm!

My name is Tallulah (from 'Bugsy Malone')

Words and Music by Paul Williams

Star Wars theme (main theme)

Music by John Williams

Mamma mia

Words and Music by
Benny Andersson, Björn Ulvaeus and Stig Anderson

Telling it how it is!